Observe and Memorize

Improve Your Mind with Sniper Observation and Memory Training

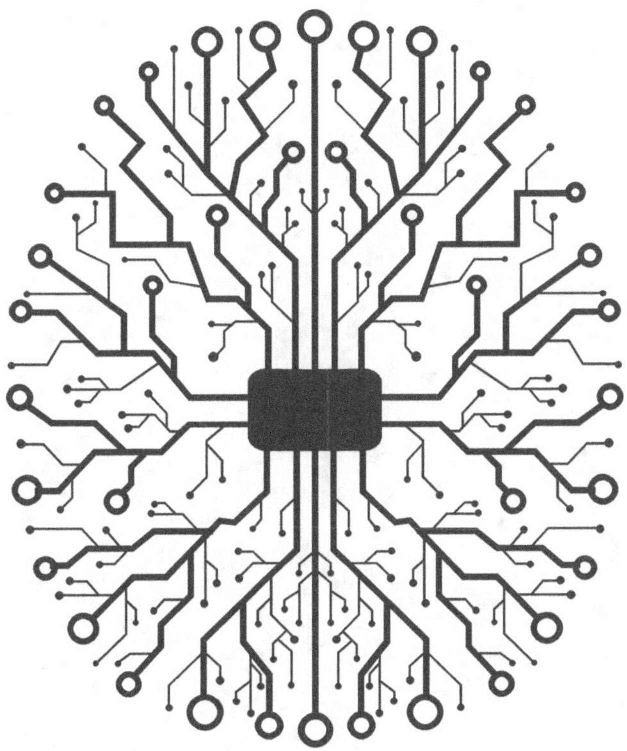

Christopher Iben

The name Kim's game comes from Rudyard Kipling's book called Kim, published in 1901. "Kim" is the story of an Irish boy who grew up in India and was trained to be a spy by the government's intelligence agency. This spy training involved improving Kim's memory. To do this, the instructors showed Kim a tray of gems and stones that he was to memorize for one minute. After the minute had transpired, they covered the tray and asked Kim how many stones he saw and what kind of stones and gems they were. Kim could memorize only a few objects at first, but eventually, he could remember not only the objects but several details about them.

Military units and even the scouts have adapted this process to train and develop memory and observational skills.

<u>How to use this book</u>:

This book contains 30 spreads (days) of increasing difficulty. Each day the observation field will have more complex elements and variations. The time spent observing the area will decrease as the time between observing and writing down what you saw will increase. The observation time and pause for the current spread will be defined on each page.

When writing down (reporting) your observations, you should always include as much information as possible, such as the total number of elements of each size, shape, color, pattern and size. You should also write down how the elements are distributed in relation to each other.

When you have finished the first 30 days, you can begin at day one again with the following added difficulties:

- Half the observation time.
- Double the pause between observing and recording.
- Turn on the TV or radio on a high volume both during observation and reporting.

Good luck.

Observation time: 60 seconds

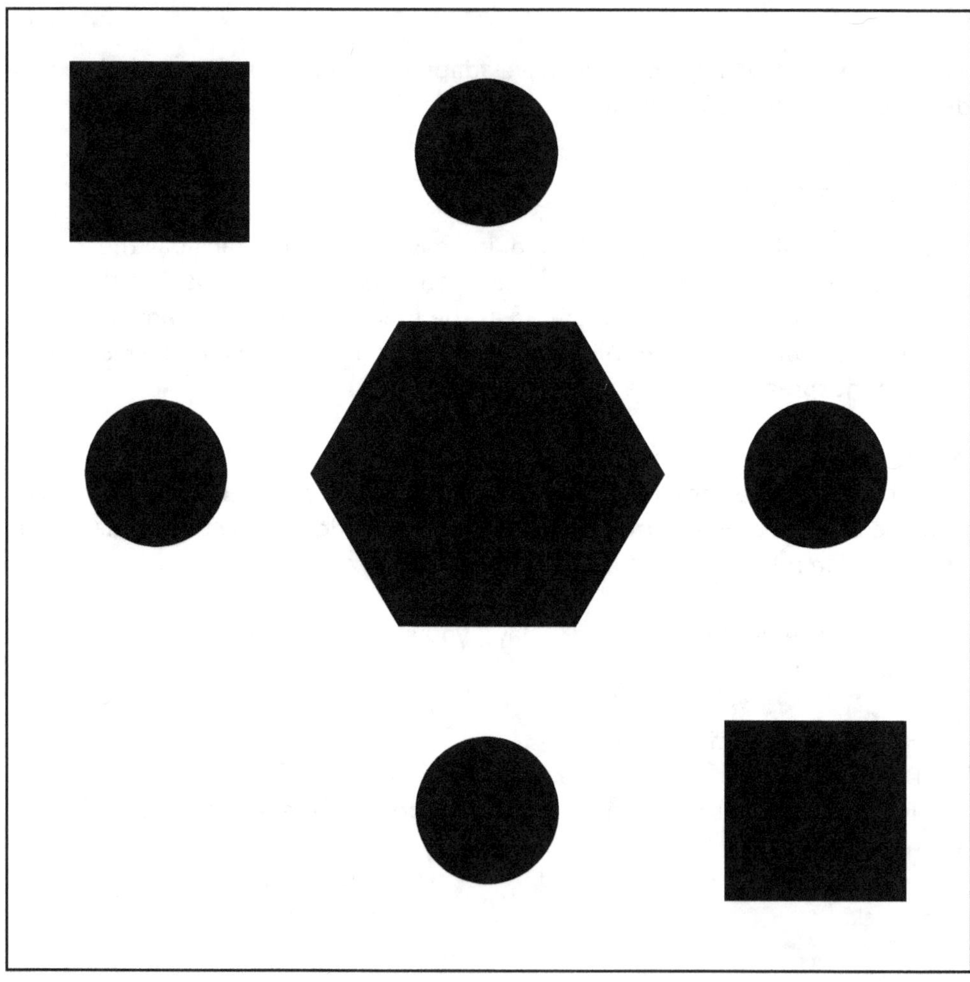

Pause: 15 seconds

1. The total number of elements according to size, shape, color, pattern and size.
2. How the elements are distributed in relation to each other.

Observation time: 60 seconds

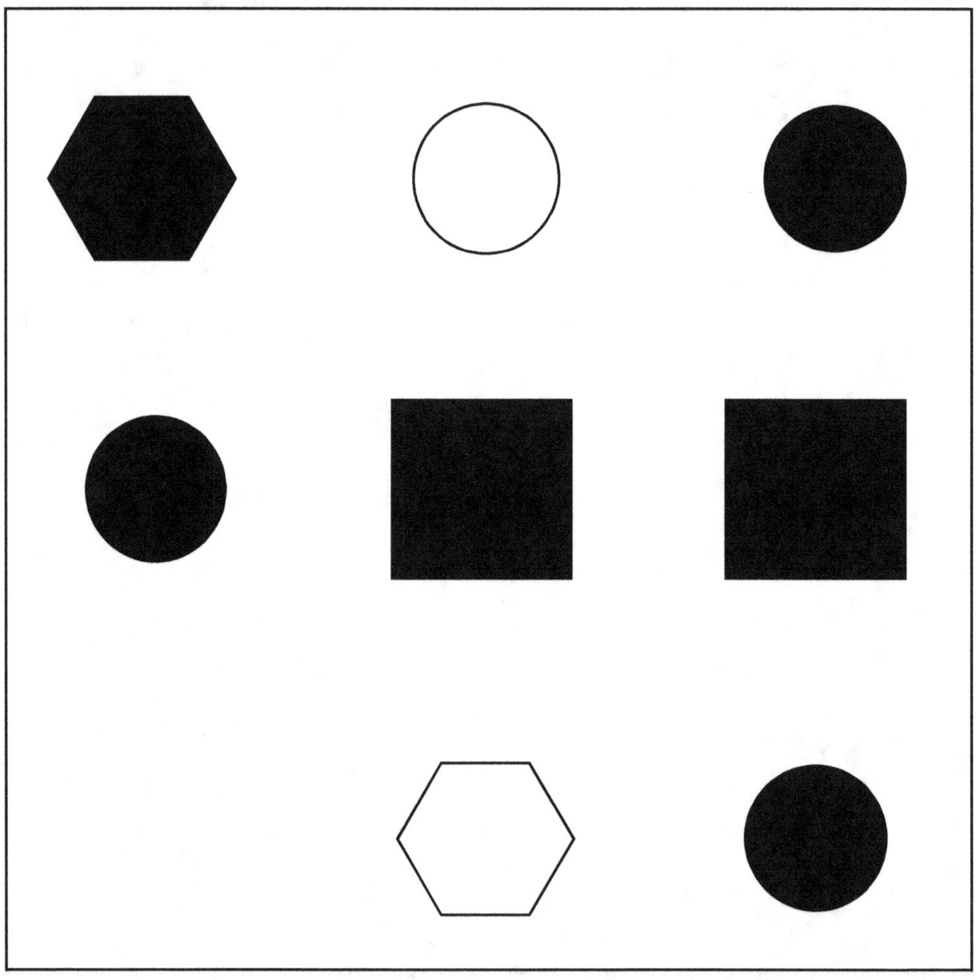

Pause: 15 seconds

Describe the scene in as much detail as possible within 1 minute

1. The total number of elements according to size, shape, color, pattern and size.
2. How the elements are distributed in relation to each other.

Report

What did I miss

Observation time: 60 seconds

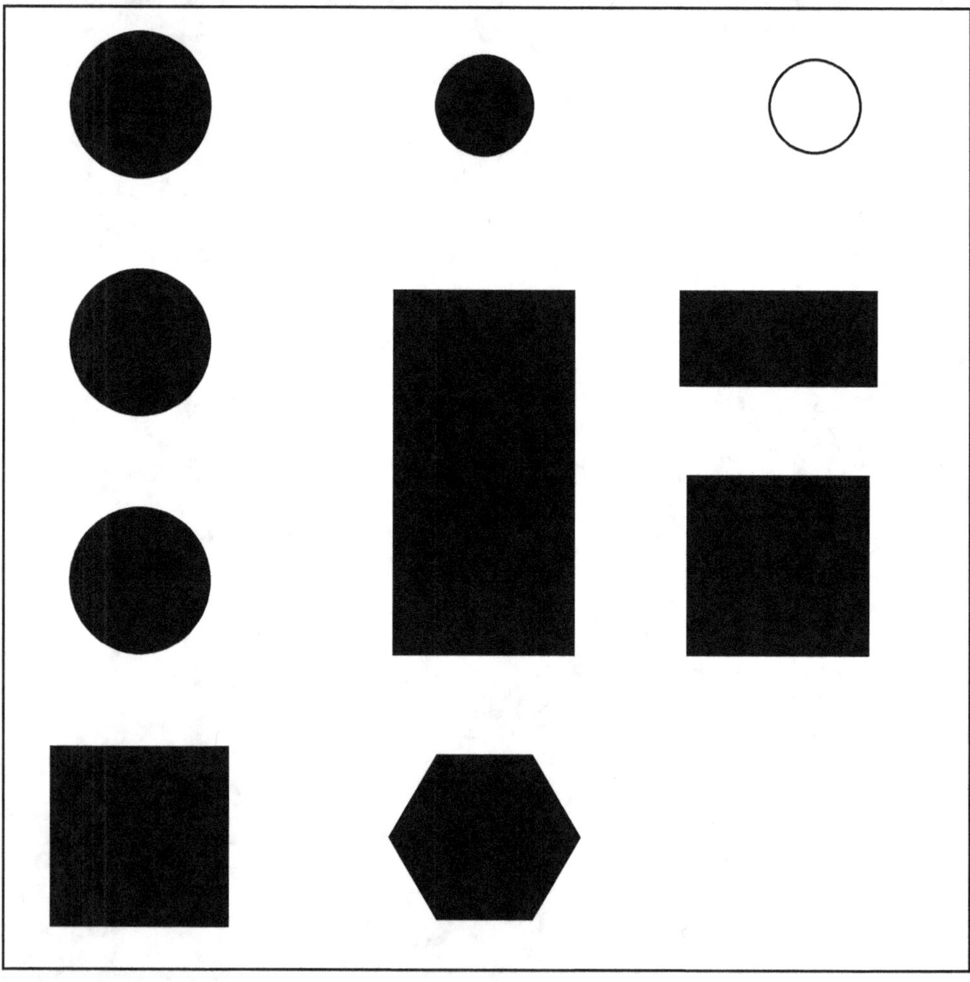

Pause: 15 seconds

1. The total number of elements according to size, shape, color, pattern and size.
2. How the elements are distributed in relation to each other.

Report

What did I miss

Observation time: 60 seconds

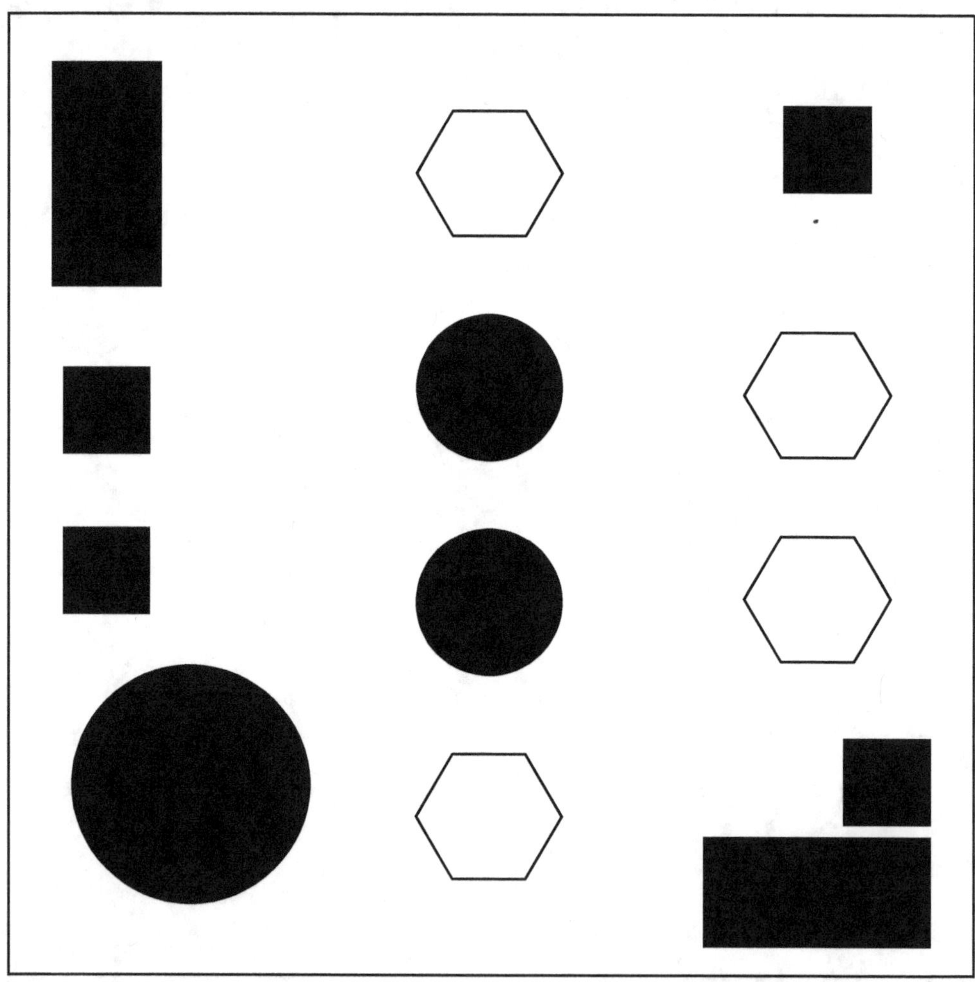

Pause: 15 seconds

Describe the scene in as much detail as possible within 1 minute

1. The total number of elements according to size, shape, color, pattern and size.
2. How the elements are distributed in relation to each other.

Report

What did I miss

Observation time: 60 seconds

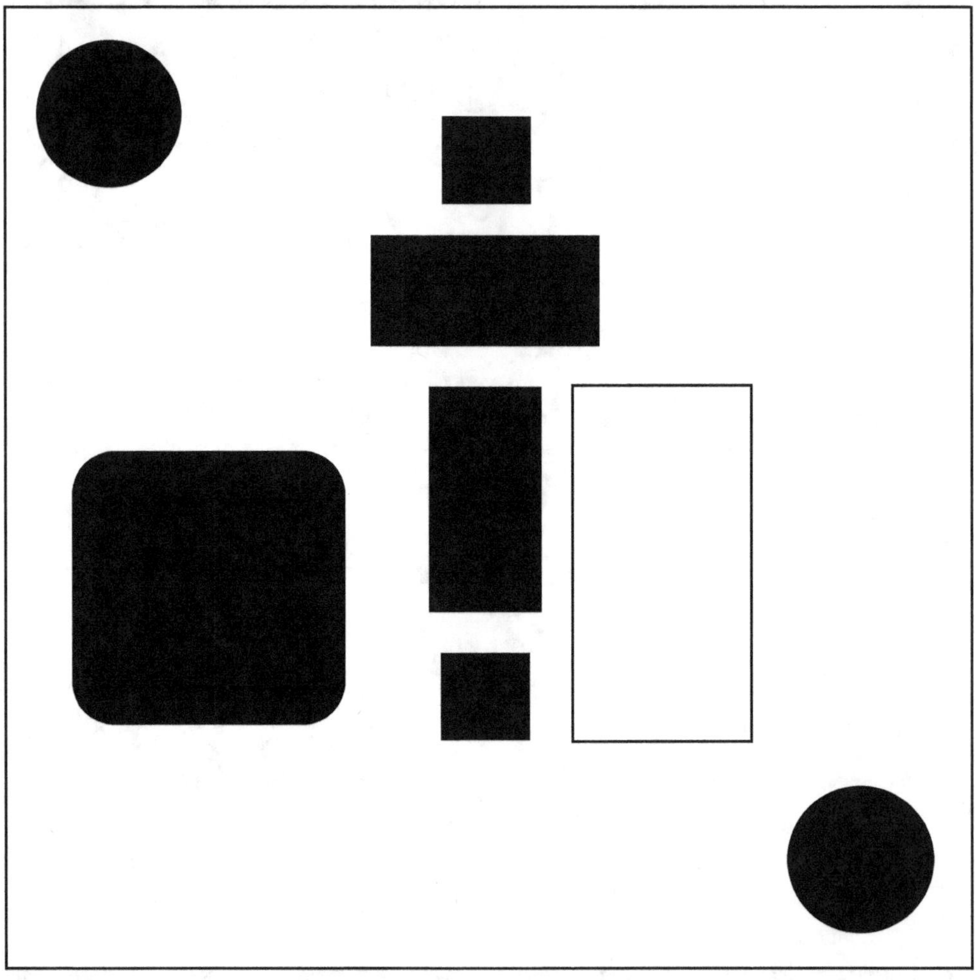

Pause: 15 seconds

1. The total number of elements according to size, shape, color, pattern and size.
2. How the elements are distributed in relation to each other.

Report

What did I miss

Observation time: 50 seconds

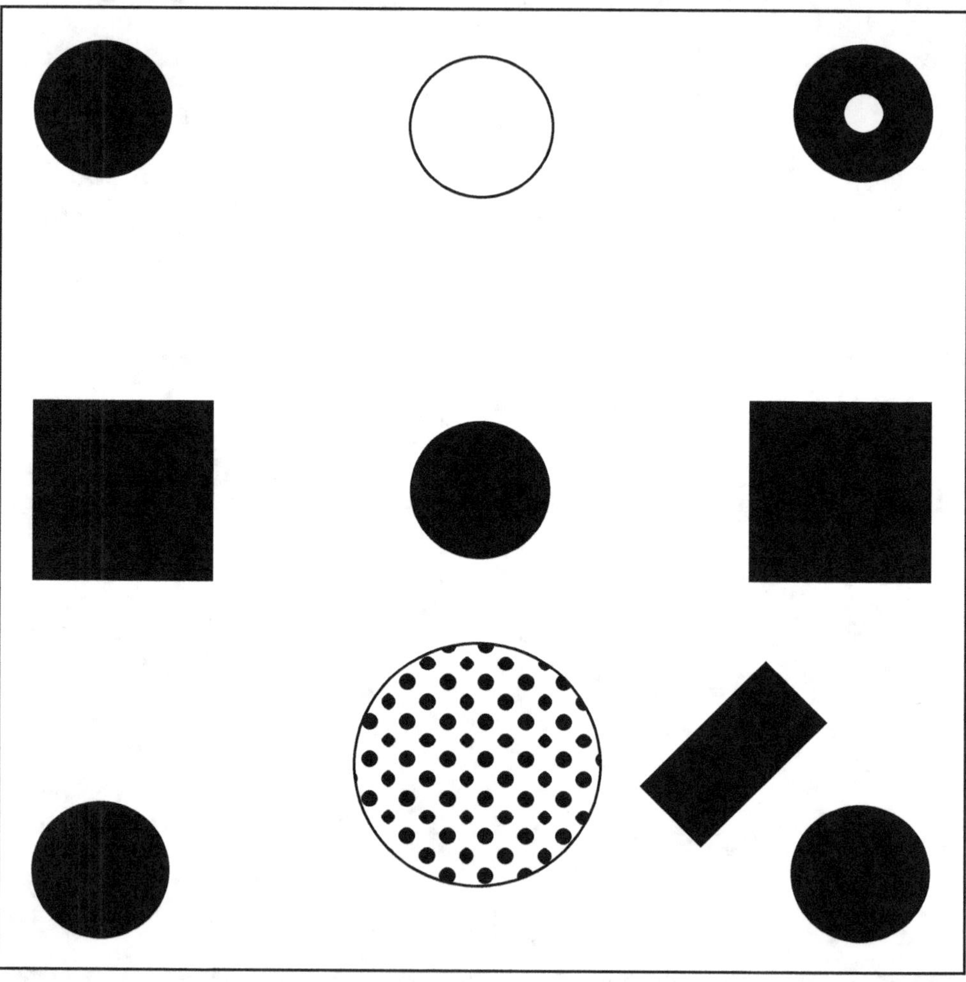

Pause: 30 seconds

1. The total number of elements according to size, shape, color, pattern and size.
2. How the elements are distributed in relation to each other.

Observation time: 50 seconds

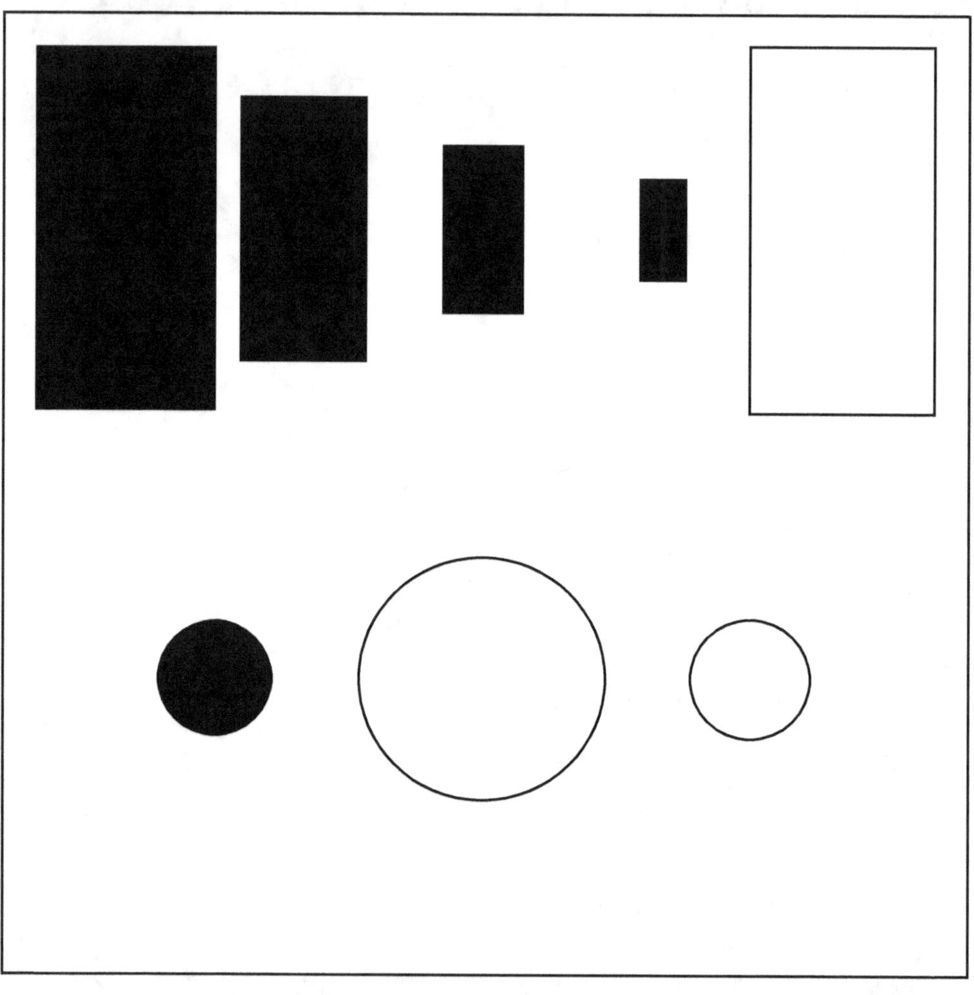

Pause: 30 seconds

Describe the scene in as much detail as possible within 1 minute

1. The total number of elements according to size, shape, color, pattern and size.
2. How the elements are distributed in relation to each other.

Report

What did I miss

Day 8

Observation time: 50 seconds

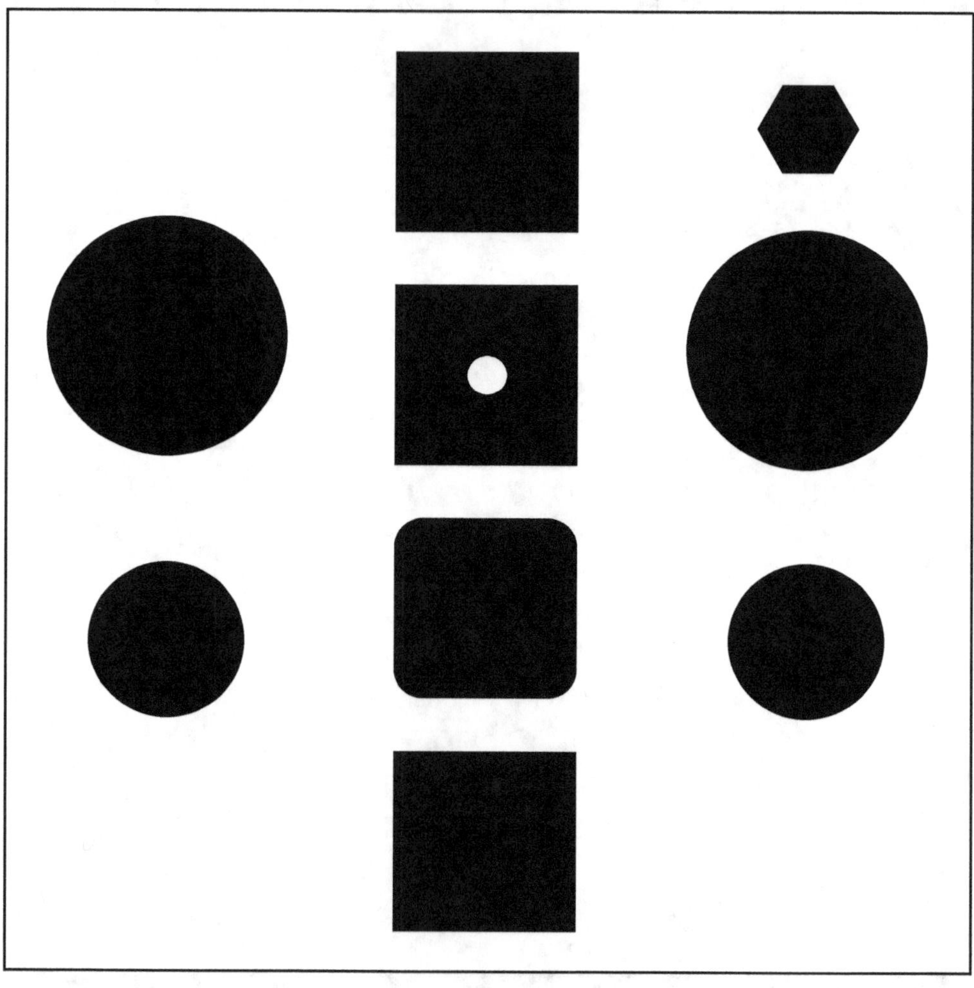

Pause: 30 seconds

1. The total number of elements according to size, shape, color, pattern and size.
2. How the elements are distributed in relation to each other.

Report

What did I miss

Observation time: 50 seconds

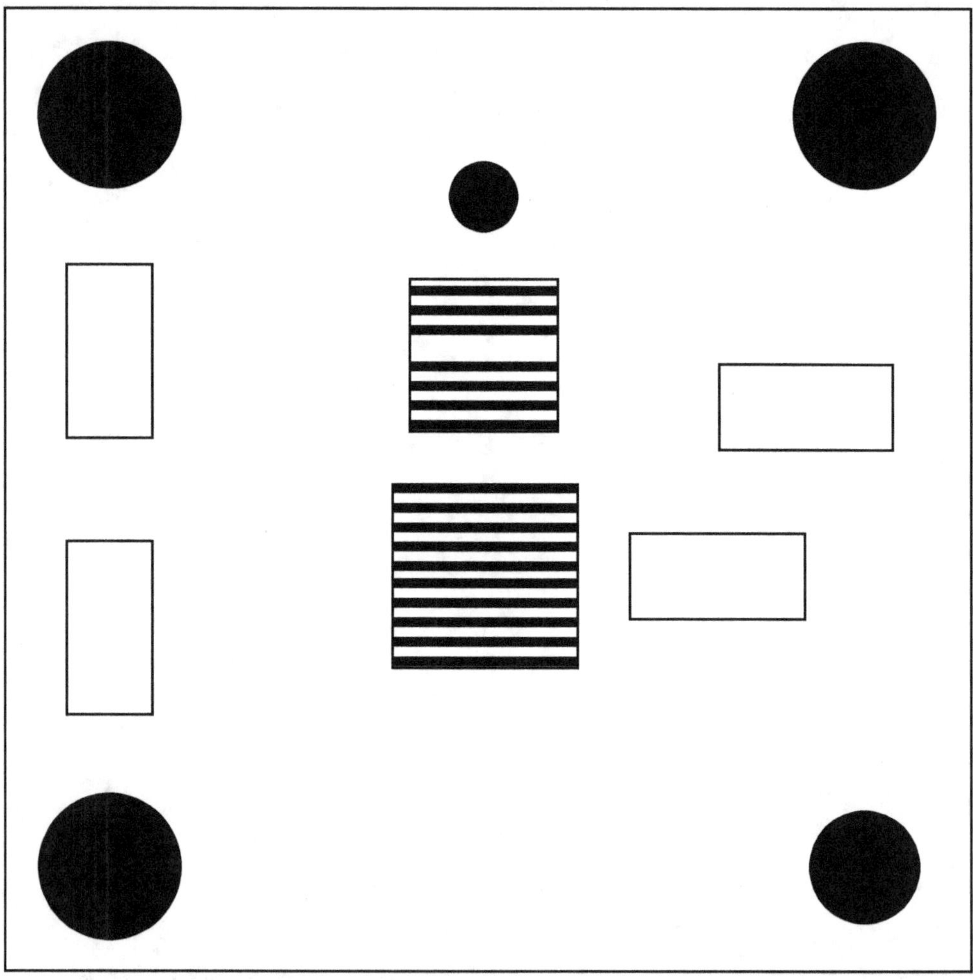

Pause: 30 seconds

Describe the scene in as much detail as possible within 1 minute

1. The total number of elements according to size, shape, color, pattern and size.
2. How the elements are distributed in relation to each other.

Report

What did I miss

Observation time: 50 seconds

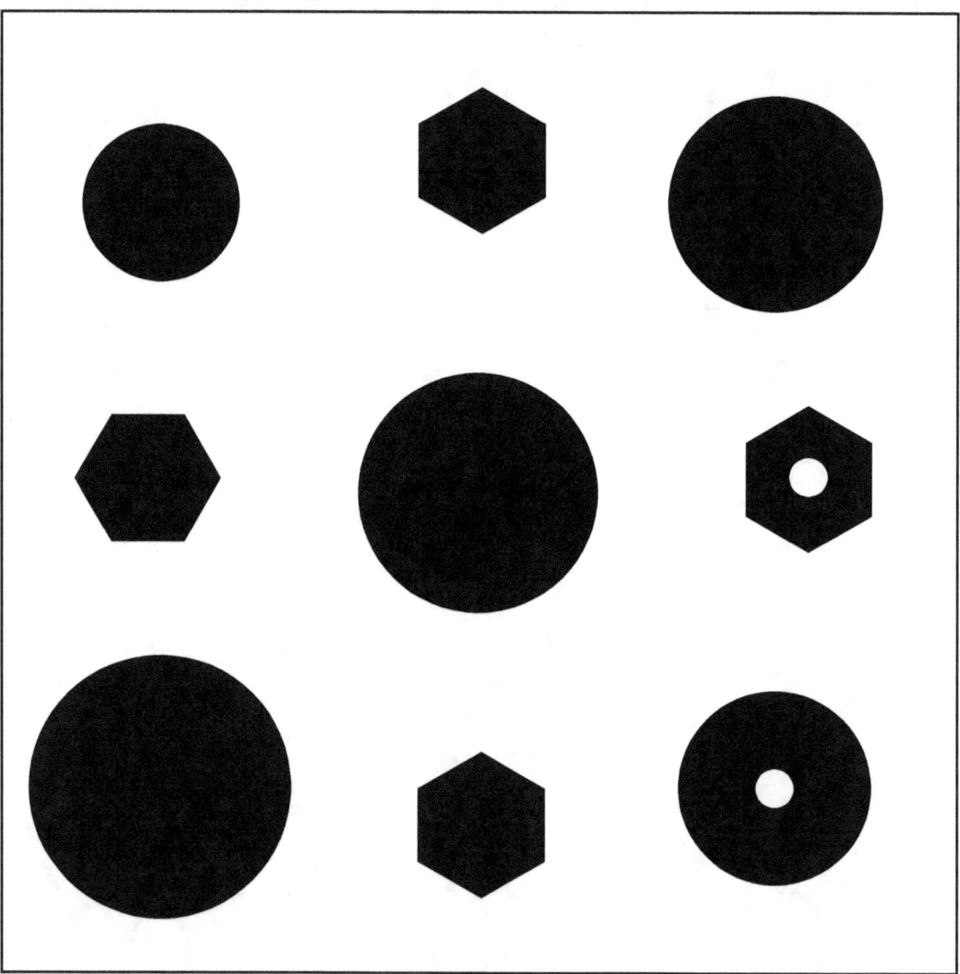

Pause: 30 seconds

Describe the scene in as much detail as possible within 1 minute

1. The total number of elements according to size, shape, color, pattern and size.
2. How the elements are distributed in relation to each other.

Report

What did I miss

Day 11

Observation time: 40 seconds

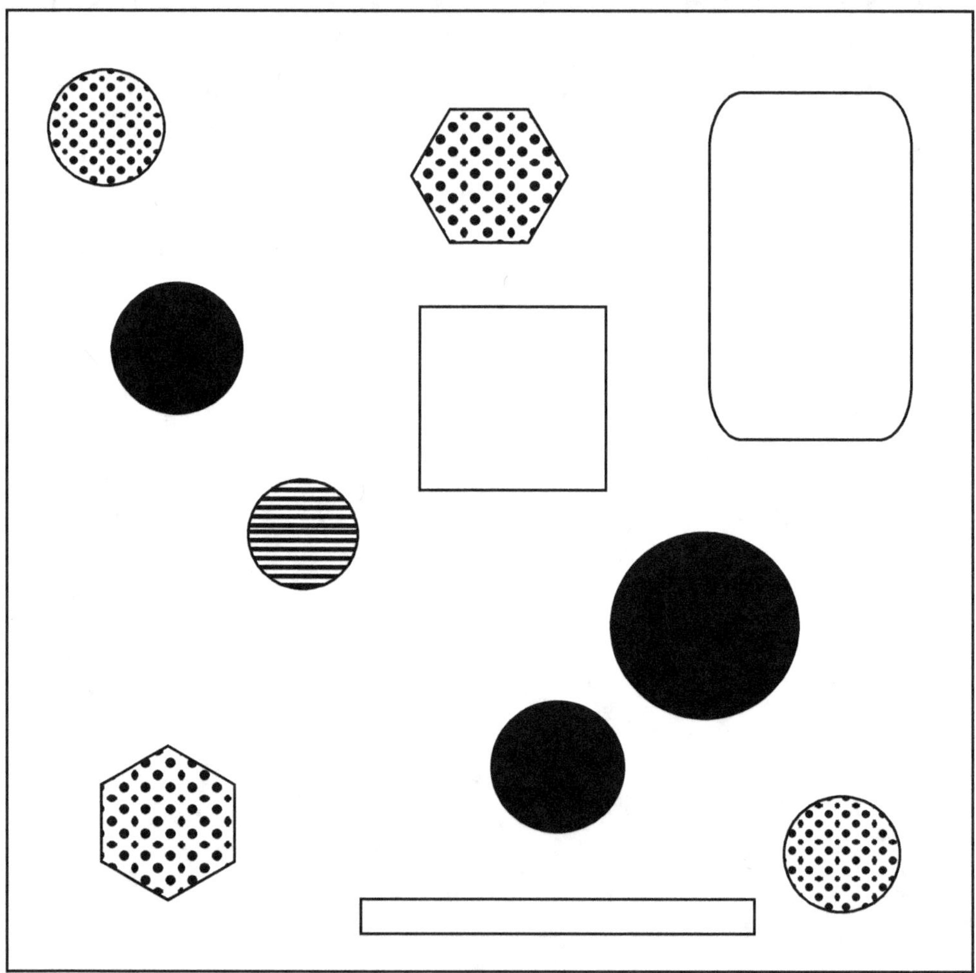

Pause: 45 seconds

1. The total number of elements according to size, shape, color, pattern and size.
2. How the elements are distributed in relation to each other.

Report

What did I miss

Observation time: 40 seconds

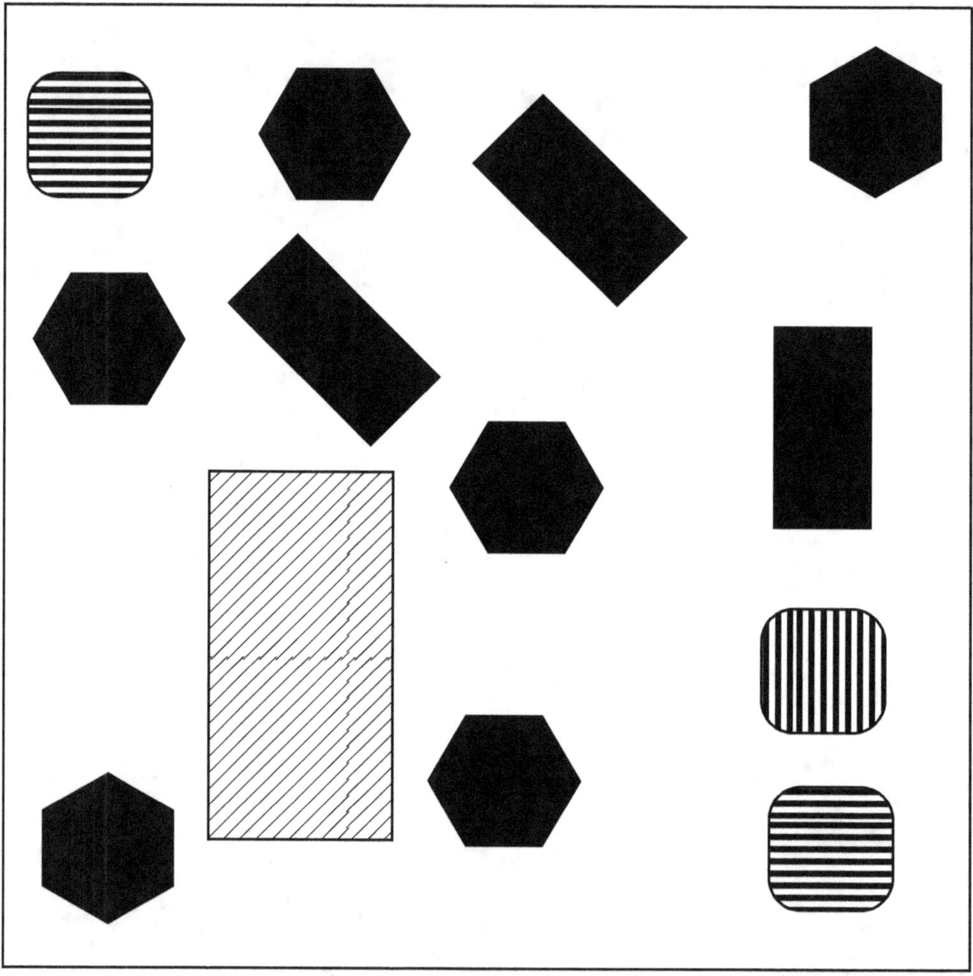

Pause: 45 seconds

1. The total number of elements according to size, shape, color, pattern and size.
2. How the elements are distributed in relation to each other.

Observation time: 40 seconds

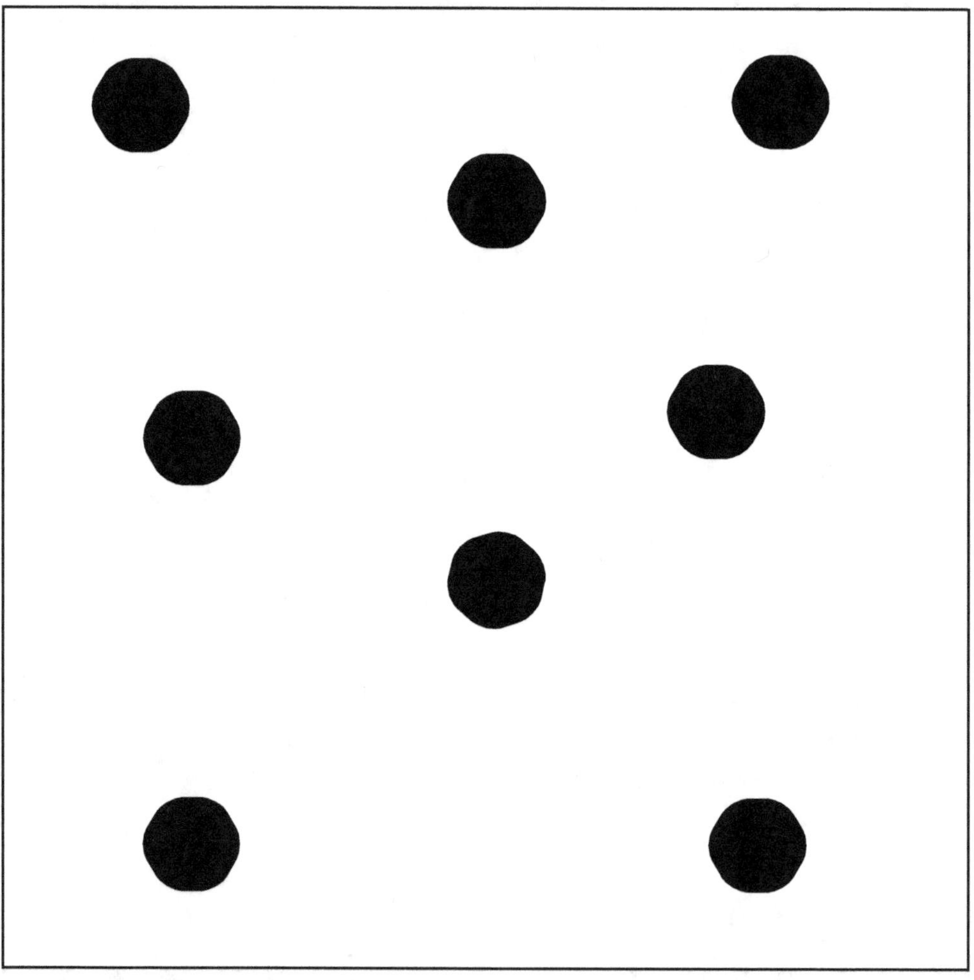

Pause: 45 seconds

1. The total number of elements according to size, shape, color, pattern and size.
2. How the elements are distributed in relation to each other.

Report

What did I miss

Observation time: 40 seconds

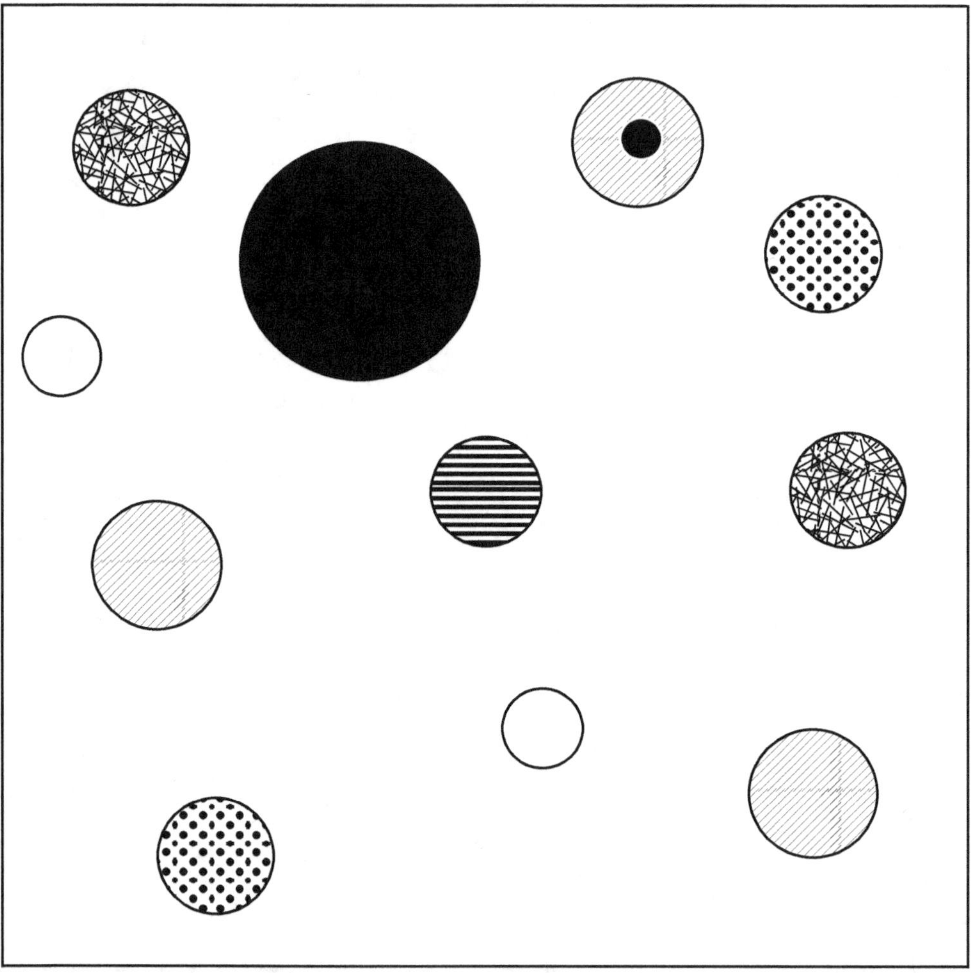

Pause: 45 seconds

Describe the scene in as much detail as possible within 1 minute

1. The total number of elements according to size, shape, color, pattern and size.
2. How the elements are distributed in relation to each other.

Report

What did I miss

Observation time: 40 seconds

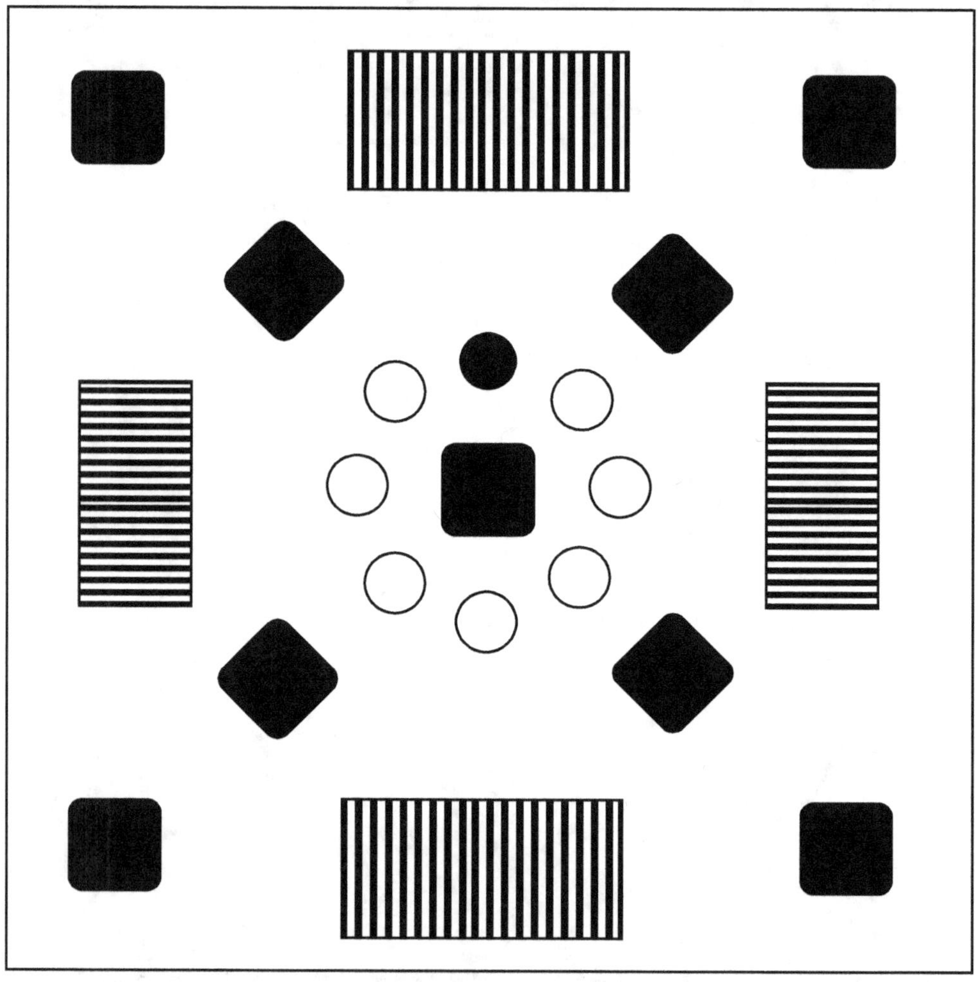

Pause: 45 seconds

Describe the scene in as much detail as possible within 1 minute

1. The total number of elements according to size, shape, color, pattern and size.
2. How the elements are distributed in relation to each other.

Report

What did I miss

Day 16

Observation time: 40 seconds

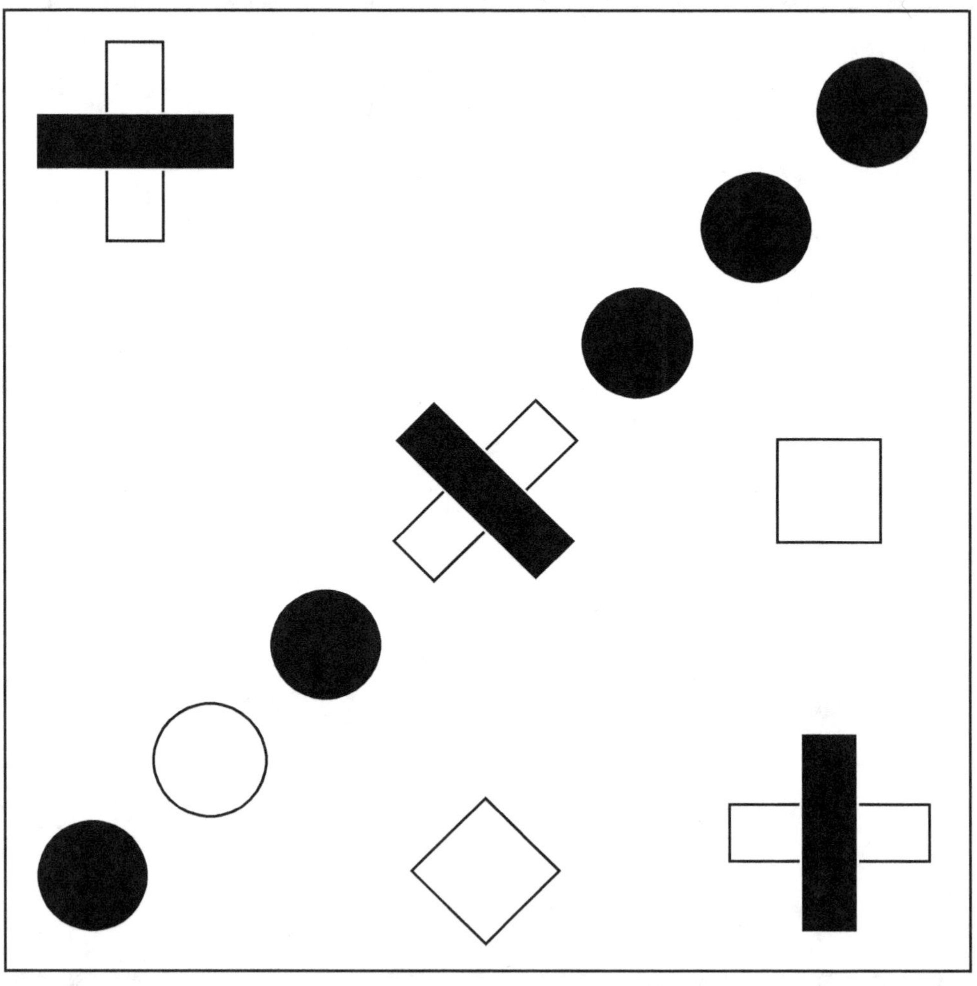

Pause: 60 seconds

Describe the scene in as much detail as possible within 1 minute

1. The total number of elements according to size, shape, color, pattern and size.
2. How the elements are distributed in relation to each other.

Report

What did I miss

Observation time: 40 seconds

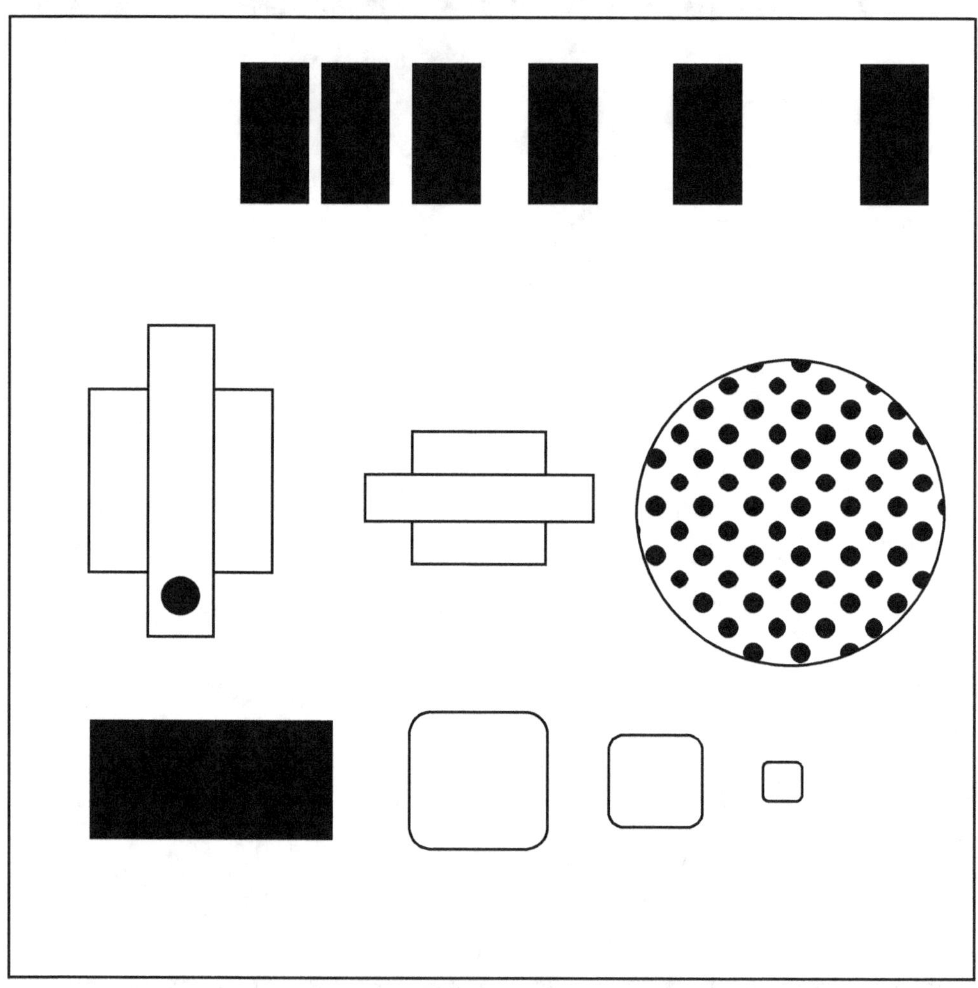

Pause: 60 seconds

Describe the scene in as much detail as possible within 1 minute

1. The total number of elements according to size, shape, color, pattern and size.
2. How the elements are distributed in relation to each other.

Report

What did I miss

Observation time: 40 seconds

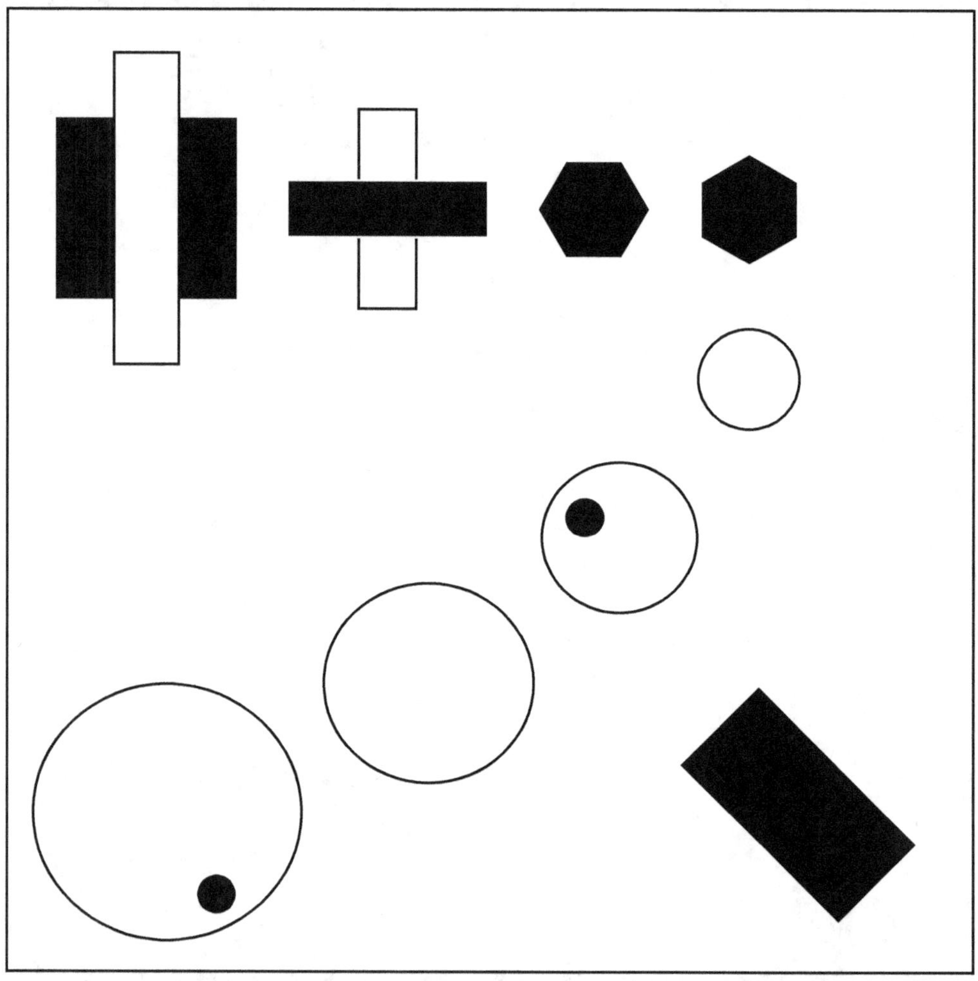

Pause: 60 seconds

Describe the scene in as much detail as possible within 1 minute

1. The total number of elements according to size, shape, color, pattern and size.
2. How the elements are distributed in relation to each other.

Report

What did I miss

Observation time: 40 seconds

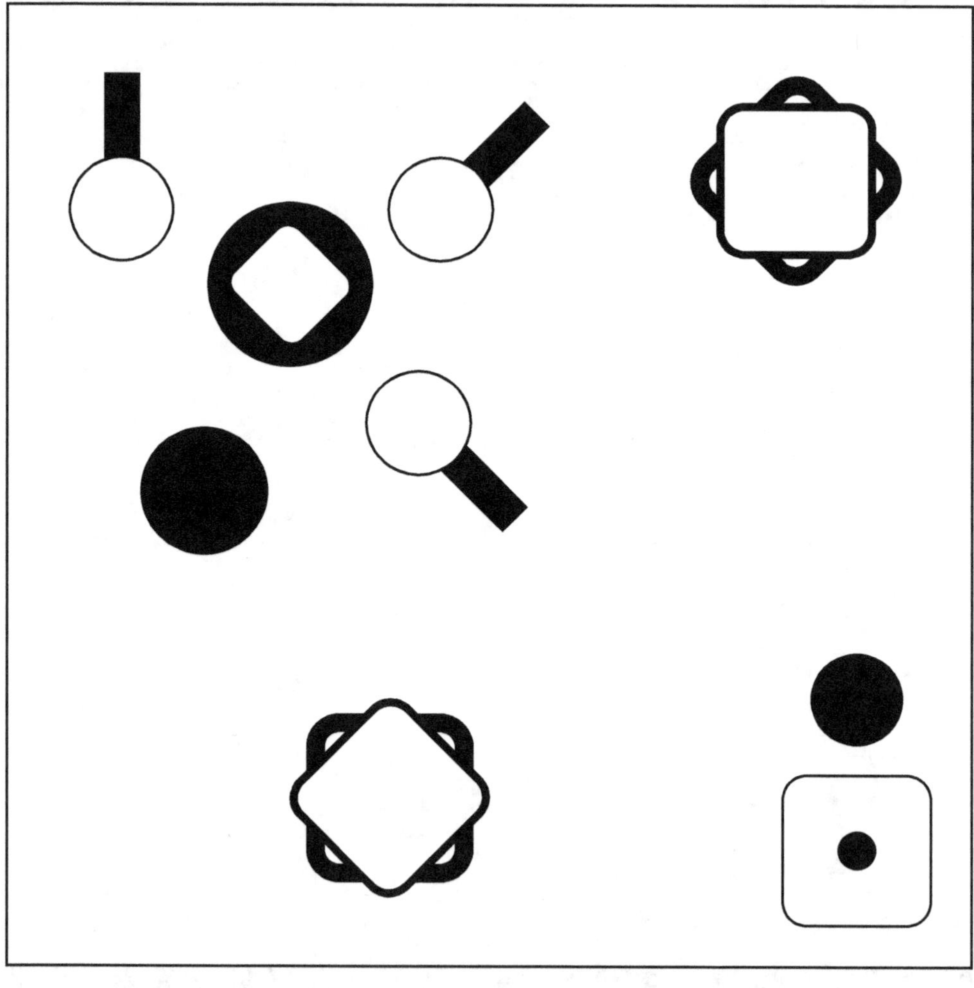

Pause: 90 seconds

1. The total number of elements according to size, shape, color, pattern and size.
2. How the elements are distributed in relation to each other.

Observation time: 40 seconds

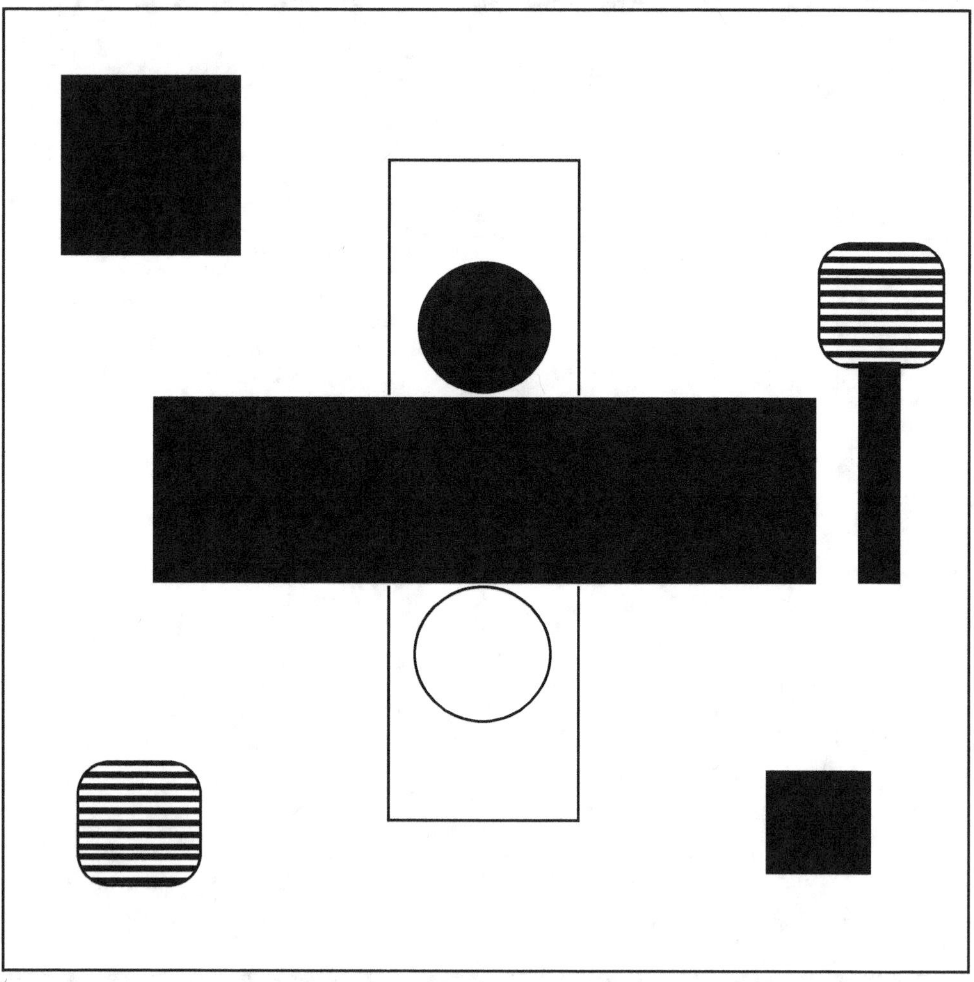

Pause: 2 minutes

1. The total number of elements according to size, shape, color, pattern and size.
2. How the elements are distributed in relation to each other.

Observation time: 30 seconds

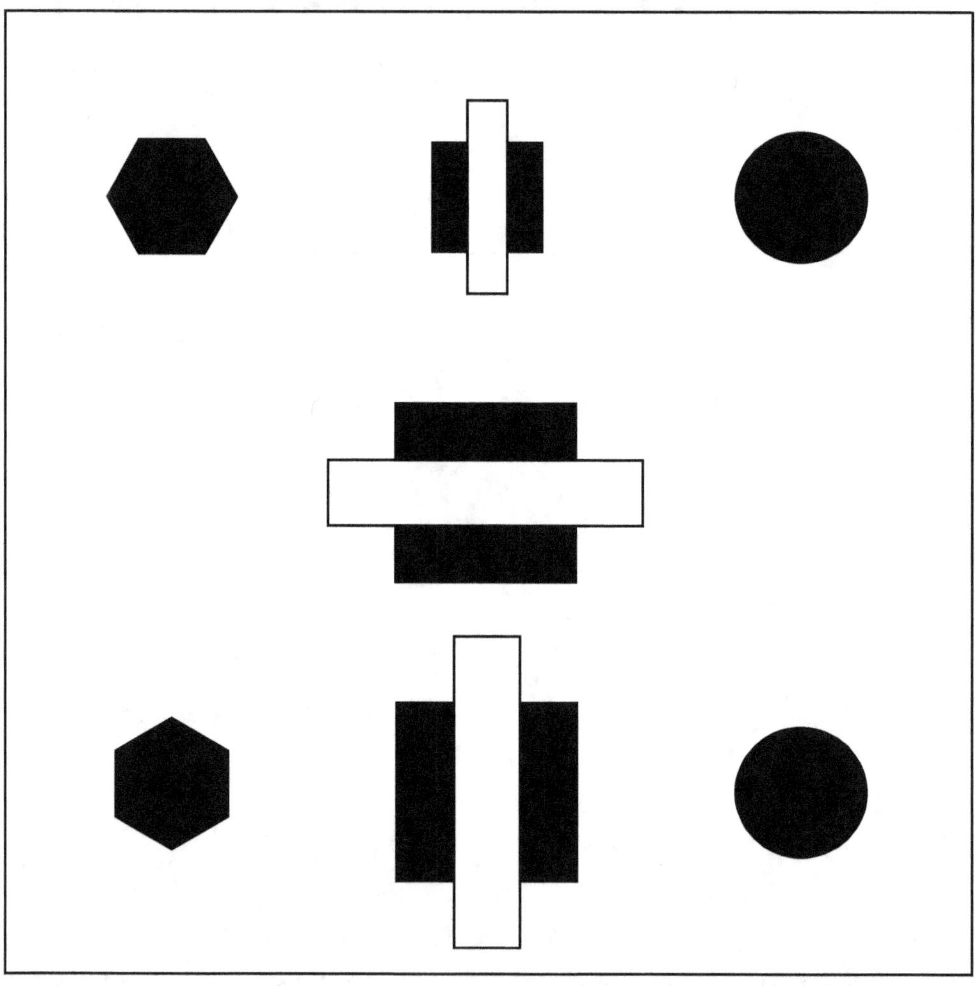

Pause: 5 minutes

1. The total number of elements according to size, shape, color, pattern and size.
2. How the elements are distributed in relation to each other.

Report

What did I miss

Observation time: 30 seconds

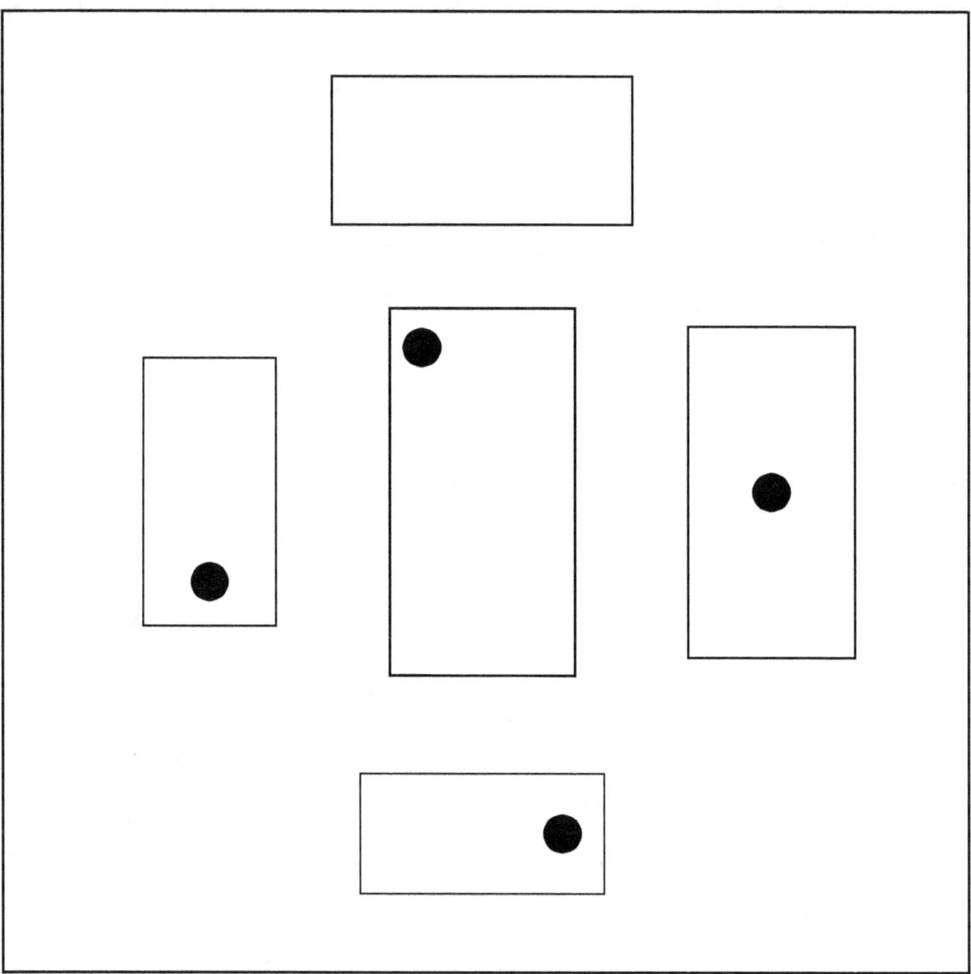

Pause: 5 minutes

1. The total number of elements according to size, shape, color, pattern and size.
2. How the elements are distributed in relation to each other.

Report

What did I miss

Observation time: 30 seconds

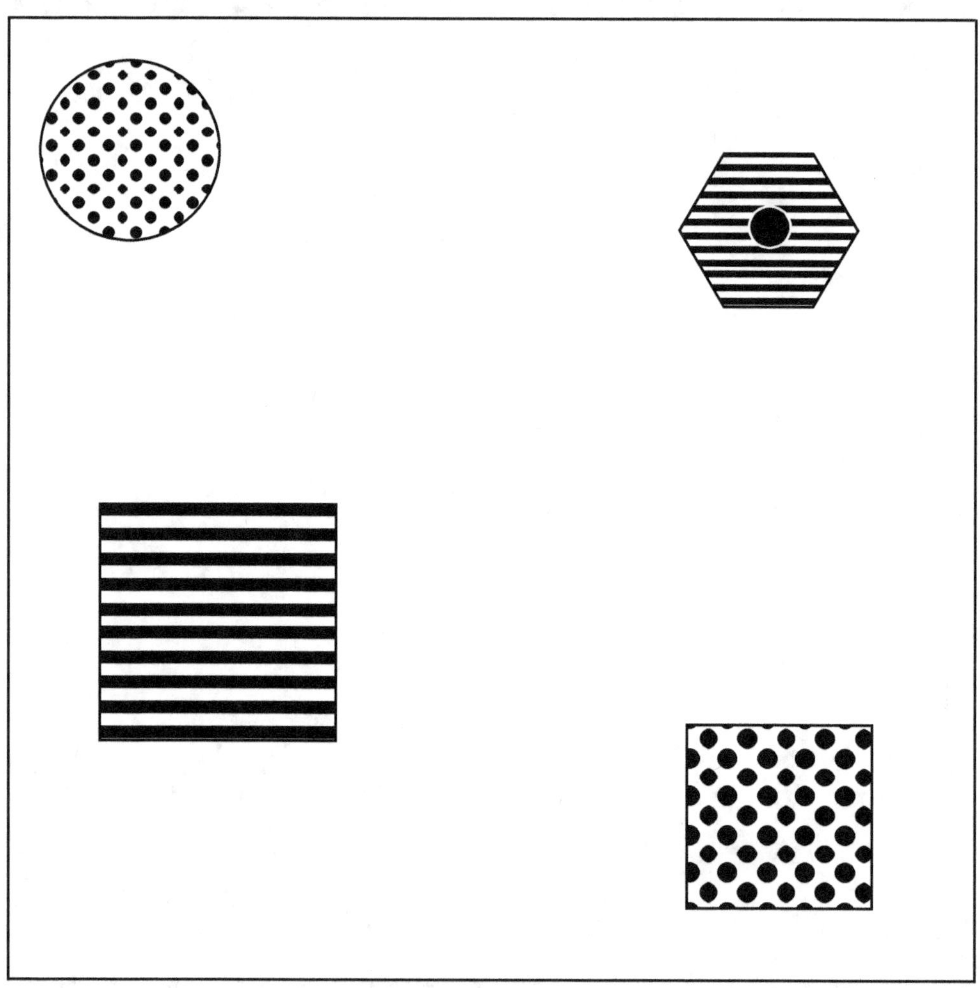

Pause: 10 minutes

Describe the scene in as much detail as possible within 1 minute

1. The total number of elements according to size, shape, color, pattern and size.
2. How the elements are distributed in relation to each other.

Report

What did I miss

Day 24

Observation time: 30 seconds

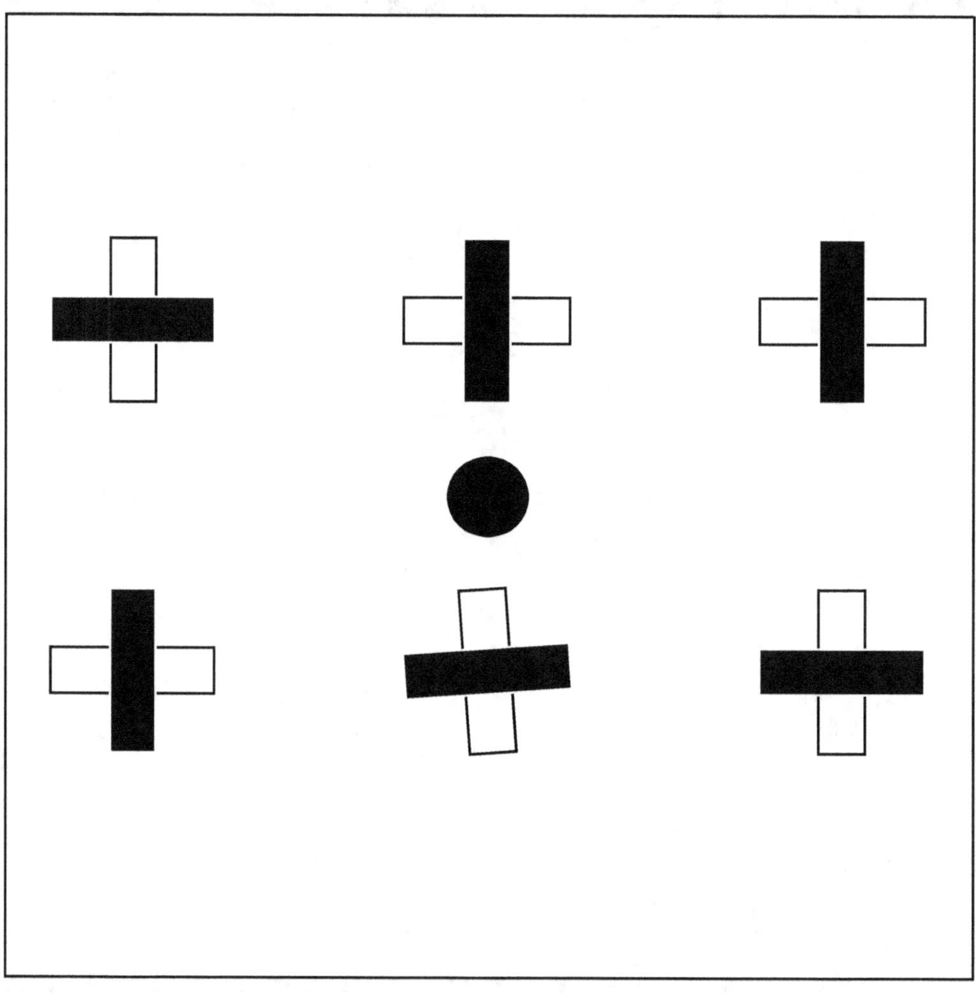

Pause: 10 minutes

1. The total number of elements according to size, shape, color, pattern and size.
2. How the elements are distributed in relation to each other.

Report

What did I miss

Observation time: 30 seconds

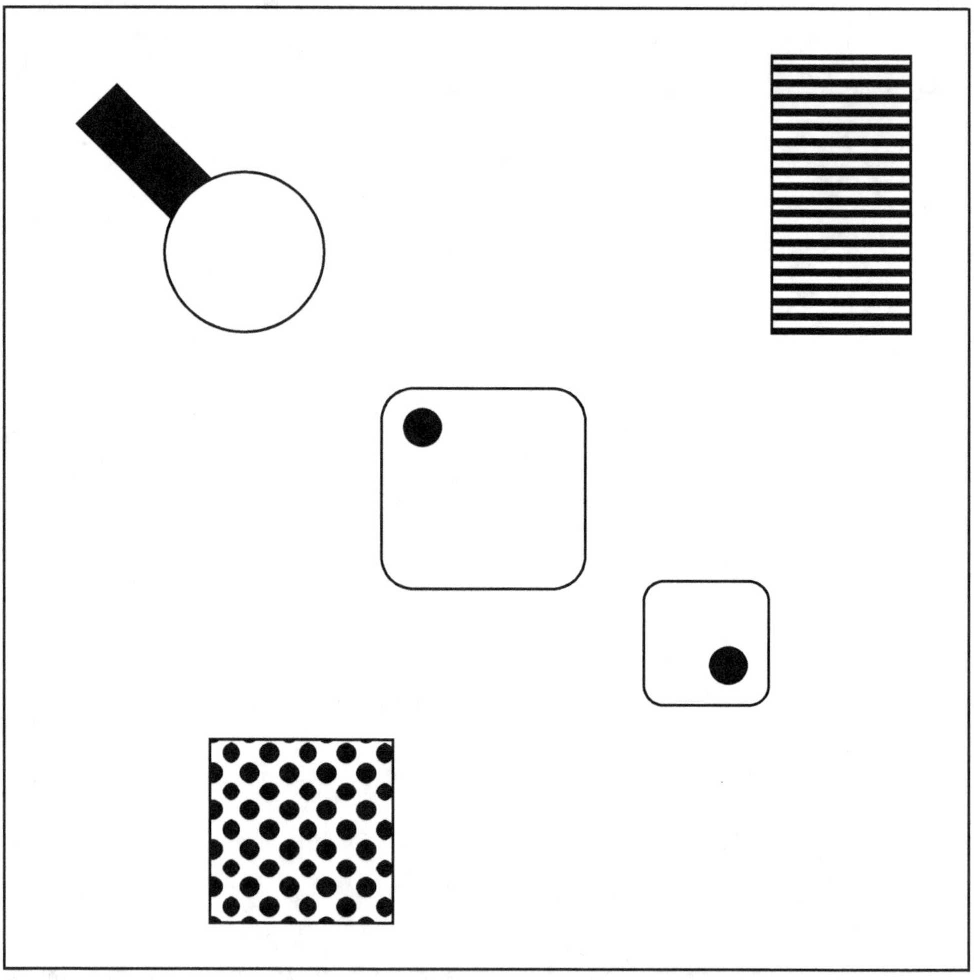

Pause: 20 minutes

Describe the scene in as much detail as possible within 1 minute

1. The total number of elements according to size, shape, color, pattern and size.
2. How the elements are distributed in relation to each other.

Report

What did I miss

Observation time: 30 seconds

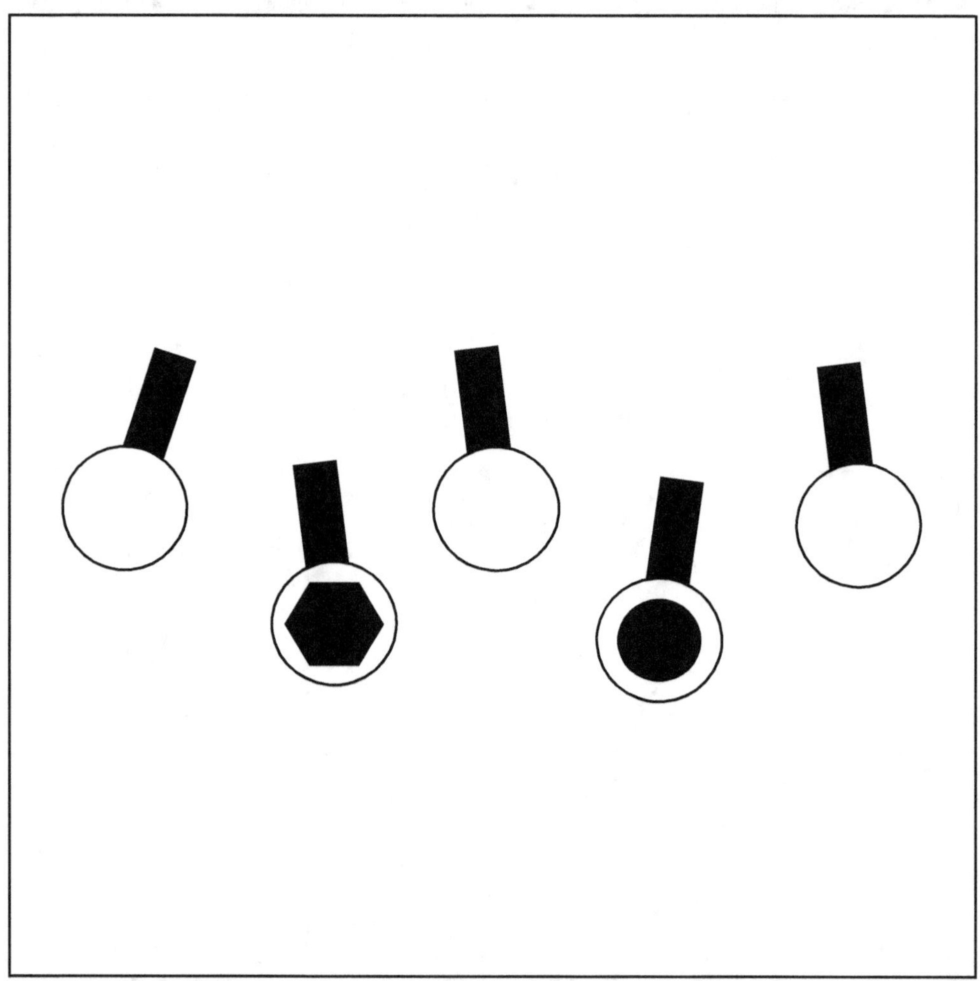

Pause: 20 minutes

Describe the scene in as much detail as possible within 1 minute

1. The total number of elements according to size, shape, color, pattern and size.
2. How the elements are distributed in relation to each other.

Report

What did I miss

Observation time: 30 seconds

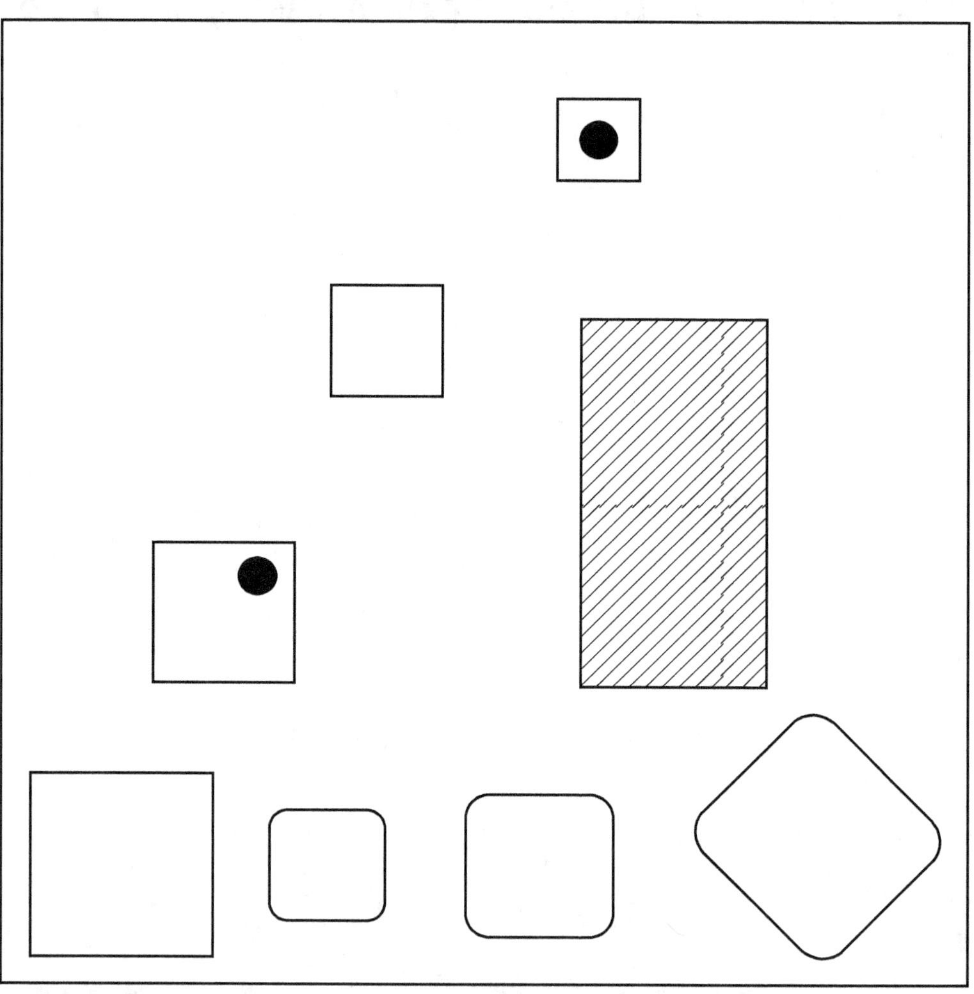

Pause: 30 minutes

1. The total number of elements according to size, shape, color, pattern and size.
2. How the elements are distributed in relation to each other.

Report

What did I miss

Observation time: 30 seconds

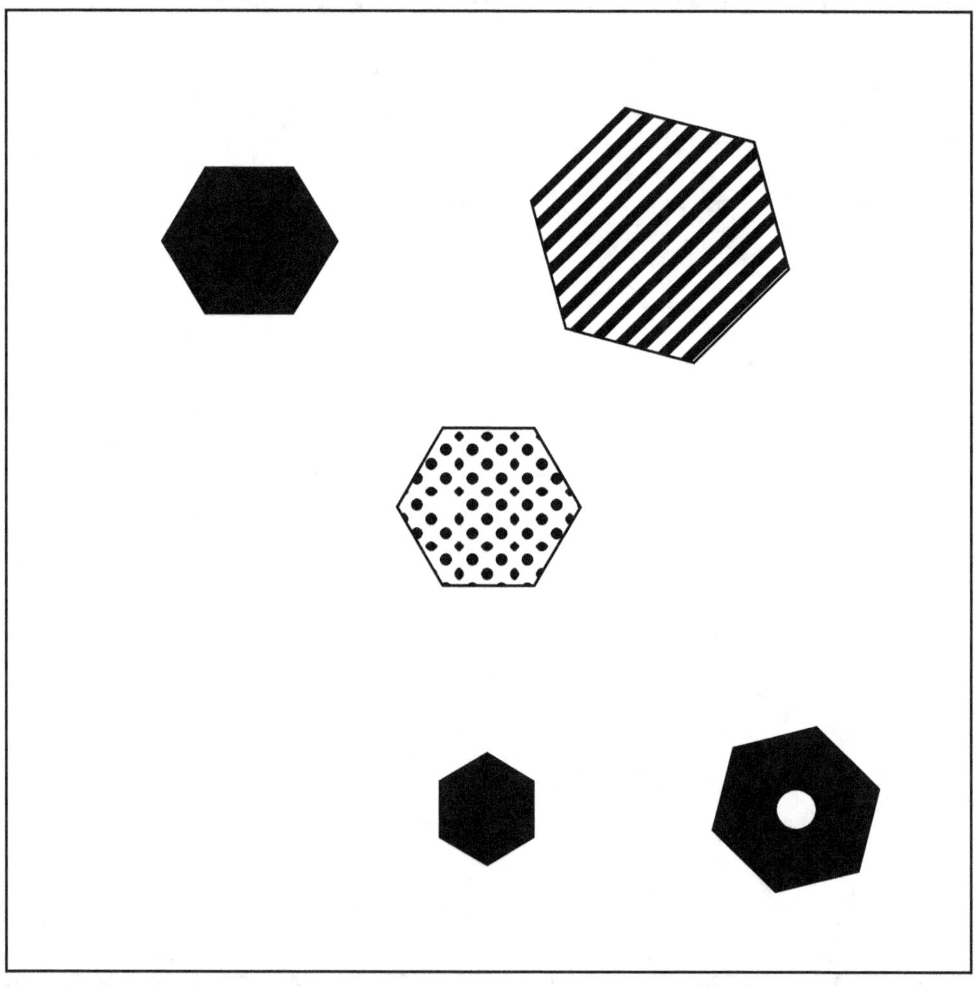

Pause: 1 hour

1. The total number of elements according to size, shape, color, pattern and size.
2. How the elements are distributed in relation to each other.

Report

What did I miss

Observation time: 30 seconds

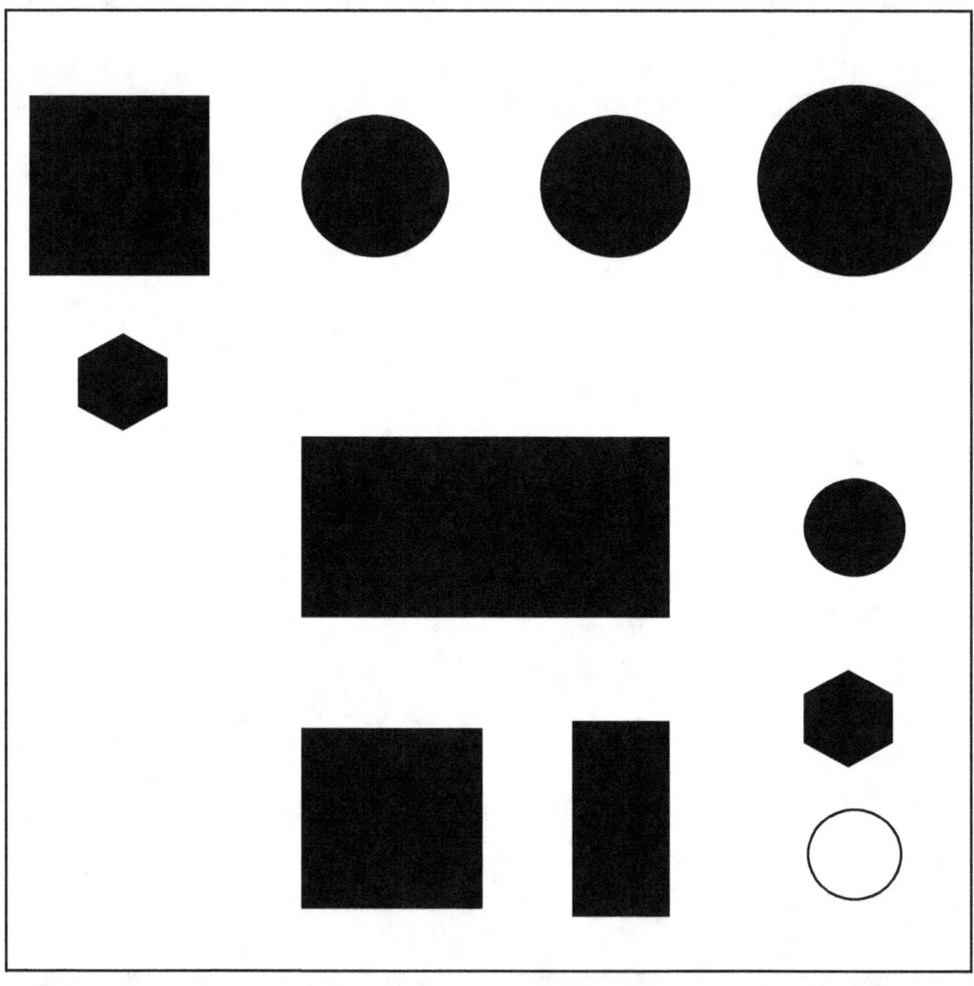

Pause: 2 hours

1. The total number of elements according to size, shape, color, pattern and size.
2. How the elements are distributed in relation to each other.

Report

What did I miss

Observation time: 30 seconds

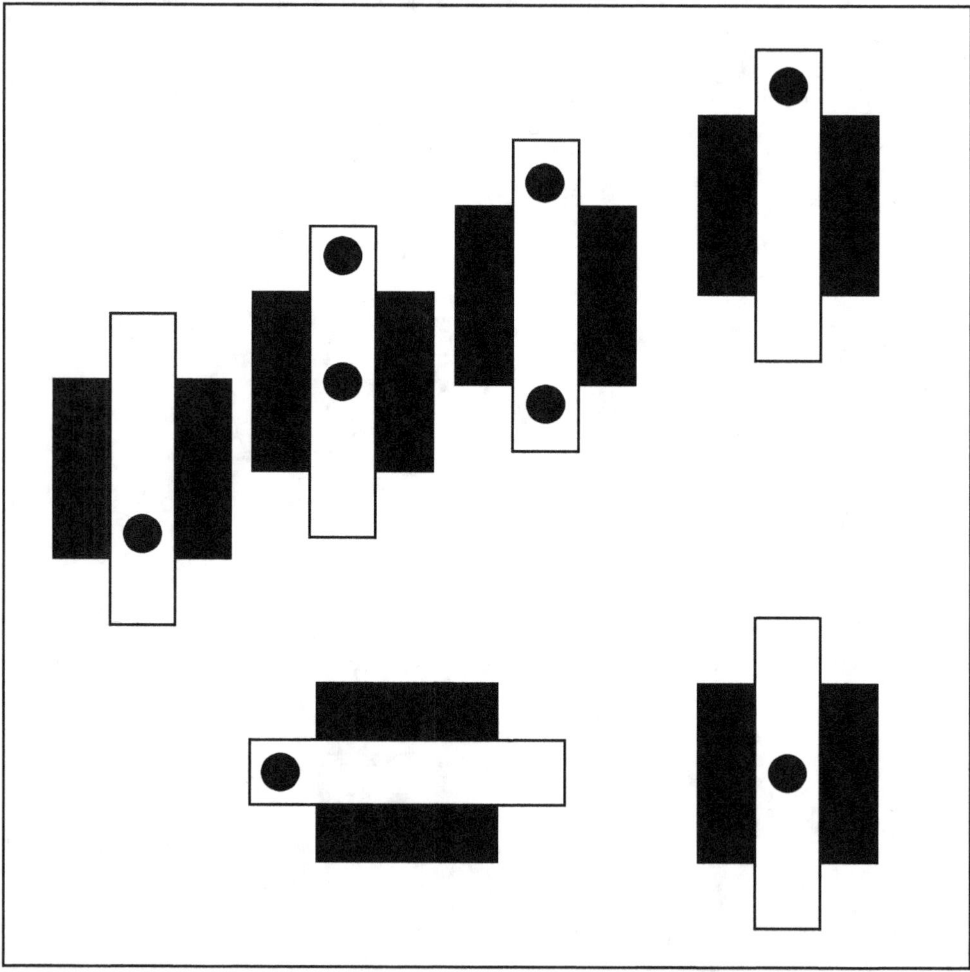

Pause: 3 hours

1. The total number of elements according to size, shape, color, pattern and size.
2. How the elements are distributed in relation to each other.